21st Century Junior Library

DISCOVER THE SABER-TOOTHED CAT

Jennifer Zeiger

Our Prehistoric World: Beyond Dinosaurs

Published in the United States of America by:

CHERRY LAKE PRESS
2395 South Huron Parkway, Suite 200, Ann Arbor, Michigan 48104
www.cherrylakepress.com

Content Adviser: Gregory M. Erickson, PhD, Dinosaur Paleontologist, Department of Biological Science, Florida State University, Tallahassee, Florida

Reading Adviser: Beth Walker Gambro, MS, Ed., Reading Consultant, Yorkville, IL

Photo and Illustration Credits: © Daniel Eskridge/Shutterstock, cover, title page; © Daniel Eskridge/Shutterstock, 5; © Daniel Eskridge/Shutterstock, 6; © estt/iStock.com, 7; © Daniel Eskridge/Shutterstock, 8–9; © Mardoz/Dreamstime.com, 10; © JA CHIRINOS/SCIENCE PHOTO LIBRARY, 11; © Vac1/Shutterstock, 12–13; © ishibashi seiichi/Shutterstock, 14; © Vac1/Shutterstock, 16–17 (all images); © ishibashi seiichi/Shutterstock, 18–19; © T_W_/iStock.com, 20; © Filipfoto25/Dreamstime.com, 21

Cherry Lake Press is an imprint of Cherry Lake Publishing Group.

Library of Congress Cataloging-in-Publication Data has been filed and is available at catalog.loc.gov.

Cherry Lake Press would like to acknowledge the work of the Partnership for 21st Century Learning, a Network of Battelle for Kids. Please visit Battelle for Kids online for more information.

Printed in the United States of America

CHERRY LAKE PRESS

CONTENTS

WHAT WAS A SABER-TOOTHED CAT?

Imagine an ancient **grassland**. A large cat crouches in the long grass. It is covered in fur, just like cats today. It has sharp claws and strong legs. Two long **canine teeth** stick out from its mouth. These teeth give the cat its name. It is a saber-toothed cat! A saber is a long, curved sword.

Saber-toothed cats would sneak up on their prey. Then they would pounce!

Saber-toothed cats were once found around the world. Europe, Asia, Africa, and North and South America had saber-toothed cats. These animals lived between 38 million and 10,000 years ago.

Saber-toothed cats had thick fur to keep them warm in colder climates.

Create!

Find out where saber-toothed cats once lived. Create a world map marking their locations. Add which kinds of big cats live in those areas today. How do you think big cat life today is different than in prehistoric times?

Some saber-toothed cats met early humans. None of these cats are alive today, though. They are **extinct**.

WHAT DID A SABER-TOOTHED CAT LOOK LIKE?

In many ways, saber-toothed cats looked like today's lions or tigers. They were covered in fur and walked on four legs. Their paws were large. Each paw had sharp claws. Some saber-toothed cats had long tails. Others had almost no tail at all.

Some scientists think saber-toothed cats roared like lions and tigers.

What do you notice first about a saber-toothed cat? Probably its two canine teeth! These teeth could be as long as 8 inches (20 centimeters)! They stuck out even when the cat closed its mouth. The cat had to open its mouth very wide to use these teeth.

Saber-toothed cats could open their jaws up to 120 degrees wide. That's 2/3 of a circle!

Think!

Other animals have really long teeth, too. Some of these animals were around thousands or millions of years ago. Others are alive today! Can you think of any? Hint: tusks are a type of tooth.

Some saber-toothed cats had short legs. These cats were heavy and strong. They were not fast, but they were good at jumping. Other saber-toothed cats were taller. They had longer, thinner legs. This helped them run fast.

A **mummified** saber-toothed cub was found in 2024 in Russia. It had been preserved by ice. It had soft, brownish-red fur.

Some scientists believe that saber-toothed cats could have had spotted coats.

Saber-toothed cats likely hunted woolly mammoths.

HOW DID A SABER-TOOTHED CAT LIVE?

Just like cats today, saber-toothed cats ate meat. They were **predators**. They usually hunted animals that were much larger than they were. These animals included horses and bison. Some saber-toothed cats may even have hunted humans.

Experts believe that some saber-toothed cats lived in **packs**. They may have cared for sick, injured, young, and old pack members. They also hunted together. This made it easier to take down very large animals.

Scientists think saber-toothed cat packs may have been similar to those of modern African lions.

Many saber-toothed cats' sharp claws retracted back into their paws when they weren't needed.

Teeth, claws, and strength made saber-toothed cats great hunters. But these features were also used for defense. Dire wolves, American lions, and other ancient predators sometimes attacked. Ancient humans may have attacked saber-toothed cats, too. The cats also fought one another over food, **territory**, and **mates**.

More than 2,000 saber-toothed cat skeletons have been found at La Brea Tar Pits in Los Angeles, California.

How do we know about saber-toothed cats? Experts study **fossils**. Fossils give clues about how an animal lived. People have found thousands of saber-toothed cat fossils. Many of them were discovered in California's La Brea Tar Pits. More fossils are found all the time. Each new fossil provides a new clue. What might experts discover next?

Ask Questions!

There are many reasons a plant or animal might go extinct. Can you think of any? Talk to a teacher, librarian, parent, or other trusted adult. Ask what they know about it. Have any plants or animals gone extinct while you were alive?

GLOSSARY

canine teeth (KAY-nine TEETH) the long, pointed teeth near the front of an animal's lower and upper jaws

extinct (ik-STINKT) no longer found living anywhere on Earth

fossils (FAH-suhlz) remains or traces of plants, animals, and other living things that have been preserved as rocks

grassland (GRAS-land) a large, open area of grass

mates (MAYTS) animals that produce young together

mummified (MUM-ih-fyed) preserved in a way that soft tissue such as skin does not rot away

packs (PAKS) groups of animals living as a unit

predators (PREH-duh-tuhrz) animals that live by hunting other animals for food

prey (PRAY) animals that are hunted by other animals for food

territory (TAIR-uh-tor-ee) an area of land claimed by an animal

FIND OUT MORE

Books

Hofer, Charles. *Siberian Tiger vs. Saber-Tooth Cat.* Mankato, MN: Capstone, 2024.

Neuenfeldt, Elizabeth. *Saber-toothed Cats.* Bloomington, MN: Bellwether Media, 2024.

Tite, Jack. *Mega Meltdown: The Weird and Wonderful Animals of the Ice Age.* New York, NY: Blueprint Editions, 2018.

Websites

With an adult, learn more online with these suggested searches.

South Carolina State Museum: FOSSIL FACTS: Saber-Cats!
Examine a fossil saber-toothed cat skull and the information scientists can get from it.

La Brea Tar Pits & Museum: Saber-toothed Cats
Learn more about the La Brea Tar Pits and saber-toothed cats.

INDEX

ABOUT THE AUTHOR

Jennifer Zeiger lives in Chicago, Illinois. She writes and edits children's books on all sorts of topics.

About Paleoartists

Paleoartists bring the prehistoric world to life! They work with scientists, paleontologists, museums, and their own research to recreate living things from long, long ago. Mark Witton is one paleoartist featured in this series. He has been studying prehistoric creatures for over 20 years! Brian Engh is another. He builds sculptures, too. He designs and builds whole exhibits. He started Living Relic Productions.